by Iain Gray

Lang**Syne**

PUBLISHING

WRITING *to* REMEMBER

LangSyne

PUBLISHING

WRITING *to* REMEMBER

79 Main Street, Newtongrange,
Midlothian EH22 4NA
Tel: 0131 344 0414   Fax: 0845 075 6085
E-mail: info@lang-syne.co.uk
www.langsyneshop.co.uk

Design by Dorothy Meikle
Printed by Ricoh Print Scotland
© Lang Syne Publishers Ltd 2015

ISBN 978-1-85217-603-7

White

MOTTO:
Loyal unto death.

CREST:
A demi-eagle atop a crown.

NAME variations include:
Whyte
Wight

Chapter one:

The origins of popular surnames

by George Forbes and Iain Gray

If you don't know where you came from, you won't know where you're going is a frequently quoted observation and one that has a particular resonance today when there has been a marked upsurge in interest in genealogy, with increasing numbers of people curious to trace their family roots.

Main sources for genealogical research include census returns and official records of births, marriages and deaths – and the key to unlocking the detail they contain is obviously a family surname, one that has been 'inherited' and passed from generation to generation.

No matter our station in life, we all have a surname – but it was not until about the middle of the fourteenth century that the practice of being identified by a particular surname became commonly established throughout the British Isles.

Previous to this, it was normal for a person to be identified through the use of only a forename.

But as population gradually increased and there were many more people with the same forename, surnames were adopted to distinguish one person, or community, from another.

Many common English surnames are patronymic in origin, meaning they stem from the forename of one's father – with 'Johnson,' for example, indicating 'son of John.'

It was the Normans, in the wake of their eleventh century conquest of Anglo-Saxon England, a pivotal moment in the nation's history, who first brought surnames into usage – although it was a gradual process.

For the Normans, these were names initially based on the title of their estates, local villages and chateaux in France to distinguish and identify these landholdings.

Such grand descriptions also helped enhance the prestige of these warlords and generally glorify their lofty positions high above the humble serfs slaving away below in the pecking order who had only single names, often with Biblical connotations as in Pierre and Jacques.

The only descriptive distinctions among the peasantry concerned their occupations, like 'Pierre the swineherd' or 'Jacques the ferryman.'

Roots of surnames that came into usage in England not only included Norman-French, but also Old French, Old Norse, Old English, Middle English, German, Latin, Greek, Hebrew and the Gaelic languages of the Celts.

The Normans themselves were originally Vikings, or 'Northmen', who raided, colonised and eventually settled down around the French coastline.

The had sailed up the Seine in their longboats in 900AD under their ferocious leader Rollo and ruled the roost in north eastern France before sailing over to conquer England in 1066 under Duke William of Normandy – better known to posterity as William the Conqueror, or King William I of England.

Granted lands in the newly-conquered England, some of their descendants later acquired territories in Wales, Scotland and Ireland – taking not only their own surnames, but also the practice of adopting a surname, with them.

But it was in England where Norman rule and custom first impacted, particularly in relation to the adoption of surnames.

This is reflected in the famous *Domesday Book*, a massive survey of much of England and Wales, ordered by William I, to determine who owned what, what it was worth and therefore how much they were liable to pay in taxes to the voracious Royal Exchequer.

Completed in 1086 and now held in the National Archives in Kew, London, 'Domesday' was an Old English word meaning 'Day of Judgement.'

This was because, in the words of one contemporary chronicler, "its decisions, like those of the Last Judgement, are unalterable."

It had been a requirement of all those English landholders – from the richest to the poorest – that they identify themselves for the purposes of the survey and for future reference by means of a surname.

This is why the *Domesday Book*, although written in Latin as was the practice for several centuries with both civic and ecclesiastical records, is an invaluable source for the early appearance of a wide range of English surnames.

Several of these names were coined in connection with occupations.

These include Baker and Smith, while Cooks, Chamberlains, Constables and Porters were to be found carrying out duties in large medieval households.

The church's influence can be found in names such as Bishop, Friar and Monk while the popular name of Bennett derives from the late fifth to mid-sixth century Saint Benedict, founder of the Benedictine order of monks.

The early medical profession is represented by Barber, while businessmen produced names that include Merchant and Sellers.

Down at the village watermill, the names that cropped up included Millar/Miller, Walker and Fuller, while other self-explanatory trades included Cooper, Tailor, Mason and Wright.

Even the scenery was utilised as in Moor, Hill, Wood and Forrest – while the hunt and the chase supplied names that include Hunter, Falconer, Fowler and Fox.

Colours are also a source of popular surnames, as in Black, Brown, Gray/Grey, Green and White, and would have denoted the colour of the clothing the person habitually wore or, apart from the obvious exception of 'Green', one's hair colouring or even complexion.

The surname Red developed into Reid, while

Blue was rare and no-one wanted to be associated with yellow.

Rather self-important individuals took surnames that include Goodman and Wiseman, while physical attributes crept into surnames such as Small and Little.

Many families proudly boast the heraldic device known as a Coat of Arms, as featured on our front cover.

The central motif of the Coat of Arms would originally have been what was borne on the shield of a warrior to distinguish himself from others on the battlefield.

Not featured on the Coat of Arms, but highlighted on page three, is the family motto and related crest – with the latter frequently different from the central motif.

Adding further variety to the rich cultural heritage that is represented by surnames is the appearance in recent times in lists of the 100 most common names found in England of ones that include Khan, Patel and Singh – names that have proud roots in the vast sub-continent of India.

Echoes of a far distant past can still be found in our surnames and they can be borne with pride in commemoration of our forebears.

Chapter two:

Saxons and Normans

There is much more colour to the name of White than it may first suggest as, peeling back the layers of history and also looking to the present day, it is revealed how bearers of the name have achieved fame and distinction.

Derived from the Old English 'hwit', indicating 'white', it came to variously refer to someone with fair hair, fair complexion, or even someone who wore white clothing.

Found from earliest times in various now redundant forms that include 'Huita', 'Huuita', 'Hwite', 'Quhyt' and 'Quhit', it is first recorded in what is now the far northern English county of Durham.

Complicating the tangled skein of genealogy for present-day English bearers of the name is that they may be of original Anglo-Saxon or Anglo-Norman stock – or a rich and colourful mix of both.

With one of the derivations of the name being from the Old English 'hwit', this indicates that flowing through the veins of some who later adopted the surname may well be the blood of those Germanic tribes who invaded and settled in the south and east of the island of Britain from about the early fifth century.

Known as the Anglo-Saxons, they were composed of the Jutes, from the area of the Jutland Peninsula in modern Denmark, the Saxons from Lower Saxony, in modern Germany and the Angles from the Angeln area of Germany.

It was the Angles who gave the name 'Engla land', or 'Aengla land' – better known as 'England.'

They held sway in what became known as England from approximately 550 to 1066, with the main kingdoms those of Sussex, Wessex, Northumbria, Mercia, Kent, East Anglia and Essex.

Whoever controlled the most powerful of these kingdoms was tacitly recognised as overall 'king' – one of the most noted being Alfred the Great, King of Wessex from 871 to 899.

It was during his reign that the famous *Anglo-Saxon Chronicle* was compiled – an invaluable source of Anglo-Saxon history – while Alfred was designated in early documents as *Rex Anglorum Saxonum*, King of the English Saxons.

Through the Anglo-Saxons, the language

known as Old English developed, later transforming from the eleventh century into Middle English – sources from which many popular English surnames of today, such as White, may well derive.

The Anglo-Saxons meanwhile, had usurped the power of the indigenous Britons – who referred to them as 'Saeson' or 'Saxones.'

It is from this that the Scottish Gaelic term for 'English people' of 'Sasannach' derives, the Irish Gaelic 'Sasanach' and the Welsh 'Saeson.'

We learn from the *Anglo-Saxon Chronicle* how the religion of the early Anglo-Saxons was one that pre-dated the establishment of Christianity in the British Isles.

Known as a form of Germanic paganism, with roots in Old Norse religion, it shared much in common with the Druidic 'nature-worshipping' religion of the indigenous Britons.

It was in the closing years of the sixth century that Christianity began to take a hold in Britain, while by approximately 690 it had become the 'established' religion of Anglo-Saxon England.

The first serious shock to Anglo-Saxon control came in 789 in the form of sinister black-sailed Viking ships that appeared over the horizon off the island monastery of Lindisfarne, in the northeast of the country.

Lindisfarne was sacked in an orgy of violence and plunder, setting the scene for what would be many more terrifying raids on the coastline of not only England, but also Ireland and Scotland.

But the Vikings, or 'Northmen', in common with the Anglo-Saxons of earlier times, were raiders who eventually stayed – establishing, for example, what became Jorvik, or York, and the trading port of Dublin, in Ireland.

Through intermarriage, the bloodlines of the Anglo-Saxons also became infused with that of the Vikings.

But there would be another infusion of the blood of the 'Northmen' in the wake of the Norman Conquest of 1066 – a key event in English history that sounded the death knell of Anglo-Saxon supremacy.

By 1066, England had become a nation with several powerful competitors to the throne.

In what were extremely complex family, political and military machinations, the English monarch was Harold II, who had succeeded to the throne following the death of Edward the Confessor.

But his right to the throne was contested by

two powerful competitors – his brother-in-law King Harold Hardrada of Norway, in alliance with Tostig, Harold II's brother, and Duke William II of Normandy.

In what has become known as The Year of Three Battles, Hardrada invaded England and gained victory over the English king on September 20 at the battle of Fulford, in Yorkshire.

Five days later, however, Harold II decisively defeated his brother-in-law and brother at the battle of Stamford Bridge.

But he had little time to celebrate his victory, having to immediately march south from Yorkshire to encounter a mighty invasion force, led by Duke William of Normandy, that had landed at Hastings, in East Sussex.

Harold's battle-hardened but exhausted force of Anglo-Saxon soldiers confronted the Normans on October 14 in a battle subsequently depicted on the Bayeux tapestry.

Harold drew up a strong defensive position, at the top of Senlac Hill, building a shield wall to repel Duke William's cavalry and infantry.

The Normans suffered heavy losses, but through a combination of the deadly skill of their archers and the ferocious determination of their cavalry they eventually won the day.

Anglo-Saxon morale had collapsed on the battlefield as word spread through the ranks that Harold had been killed.

Amidst the carnage of the battlefield, it was difficult to identify Harold – the last of the Anglo-Saxon kings.

Some sources assert William ordered his body to be thrown into the sea, while others state it was secretly buried at Waltham Abbey.

What is known with certainty, however, is that William in celebration of his great victory founded Battle Abbey, near the site of the battle, ordering that the altar be sited on the spot where Harold was believed to have fallen.

William was declared King of England on December 25, and the complete subjugation of his Anglo-Saxon subjects followed.

Those Normans who had fought on his behalf were rewarded with the lands of Anglo-Saxons, many of whom sought exile abroad as mercenaries.

Among those Normans who flocked to England in the wake of the Conquest was a family of

Le Blancs ('the Whites'), who were rewarded with lands in Co. Durham.

Within an astonishingly short space of time, Norman manners, customs and law were imposed on England – laying the basis for what subsequently became established 'English' custom and practice.

But beneath the surface, old Anglo-Saxon culture was not totally eradicated, with some aspects absorbed into those of the Normans, while faint echoes of the Anglo-Saxon past is still seen today in the form of popular surnames such as White.

Chapter three:

Honours and fame

Across the Atlantic, Whites quite literally gained an early foothold on the shores of North America.

This was through Peregrine White, the first English child born to the Pilgrims in the New World.

His mother gave birth to him shortly before the Pilgrim's ship, *Mayflower*, docked at Provincetown Harbor, in Provincetown, Massachusetts, in November 1620, and he was named Peregrine because the name denotes 'one who journeys to foreign lands', or 'pilgrim'.

Not much is known of his later life, although he is understood to have held a number of civil and military posts before his death in Massachusetts in 1703.

There is a record, however, of him and his future wife Susan being fined by the Puritanical authorities 'for fornication before marriage or contract.'

The couple later married and went on to have seven children.

Another early New World pioneer of the

name of White was James White, born in 1747 in Rowan County, North Carolina.

Serving as a captain in the North Carolina militia during the American Revolutionary War of 1775 to 1783, it was he who founded White's Fort, later Knoxville, Tennessee, before his death in 1821.

Another American 'founder' was Andrew Dickson White, the diplomat and historian who was born in Homer, New York City, in 1832 and who died in 1918.

The son of a wealthy banker, it was he who, along with the entrepreneur Ezra Cornell, co-founded the centre of academic excellence known today as Cornell University, serving as its first president from 1866 to 1885.

In more contemporary times, a pioneer of a different sort, this time of space exploration, was Lieutenant Colonel Edward White, better known as Ed White, the U.S. Air Force officer and NASA astronaut who, on June 3, 1965, became the first American to conduct a spacewalk.

Born in 1930 in San Antonio, Texas, he was among three astronauts killed in January of 1967 in a fire that broke out during a training exercise at the Kennedy Space Center at Cape Canaveral.

Bearers of the White name have also gained distinction on the battlefield.

Born Jacob Weiss in Leeds, Yorkshire, in 1896, the son of Jewish immigrants from Russia, Jack White was a First World War recipient of the Victoria Cross (VC), the highest award for bravery in the face of enemy action for British and Commonwealth forces.

He had been a private with the 6th King's Own Royal Regiment (Lancaster), when, in action in March 1917 at the Dialah River, Mesopotamia, he used a pontoon to ferry wounded comrades to safety across the river.

Later promoted to Lance Corporal, he was refused permission to enlist in Britain's Home Guard during the Second World War, because the nit-picking and small-minded authorities claimed his parents had failed to be properly naturalised as British citizens – this despite the fact that he had been born in Yorkshire and was a holder of the VC.

Field Marshall Sir George White, born in 1835 at Port Stewart, Co. Londonderry, and who died in 1912, was an Irish recipient of the VC.

He had been second in command of the 92nd Regiment (later the Gordon Highlanders) during the Second Anglo-Afghan War when, in October of 1879, he led a successful personal assault, armed only with a rifle, on a fortified hill.

He shot the enemy leader, while the rest panicked and fled.

Later appointed Commander-in-Chief, India, he died in 1912, while his son, Jack White, was the Irish Republican who in 1913 co-founded the Irish Citizen Army along with James Connolly.

In politics, James Whyte was the Scots-Australian politician who was born in 1820 near Greenlaw, Berwickshire, in the Scottish Borders, and who died in 1882.

Immigrating in 1832 to what was then Van Diemen's Land, now Tasmania, he served as 6th Premier of Tasmania from 1863 to 1866.

In the realms of political activism, Walter White, born in 1893 in Atlanta, Georgia, was the distinguished African-American who served as executive secretary from 1931 until his death in 1955 of the National Association for the Advancement of Coloured People.

In Canada, William Andrew White III, better known as Bill White, was the composer and activist for social justice who was born in 1915 in Truro, Nova Scotia.

In 1949 he became the first black Canadian to run for federal office, as the Co-operative and Commonwealth Federation candidate for the Spadina constituency.

He was appointed an Officer of the Order of Canada eleven years before his death in 1981, for services to the community and his contribution to better relations and understanding between peoples of different racial background.

It is perhaps apt that, bearing in mind their own historical roles, bearers of the White name have also been noted recorders of some of the most momentous events in history.

Born in 1904 in the Bronx district of New York, Margaret Bourke-White was the renowned American photographer who had a special gift of being in the right place at the right time.

Appointed associate editor of *Fortune* magazine in 1929, a year later she became the first Western photographer allowed into the Soviet Union, and was later hired as *Life* magazine's first female staff photographer.

She recorded stark images of drought victims of America's Dust Bowl during the mid-1930s, while during the Second World War she became the first female war correspondent and the first woman allowed into combat zones.

Known as "Maggie the Indestructible" by her *Life* magazine colleagues, she survived many dangerous encounters, and at the close of the war had the grim task of photographing the horror of the newly liberated Buchenwald concentration camp.

Her camera was also to hand in 1948 when the great Indian patriot, moral teacher and social reformer Mahatma Gandhi was assassinated while en route to a prayer meeting.

Her autobiographical *Portrait of Myself* was published eight years before her death in 1971, and she was portrayed by the actress Candice Bergen in the 1982 film *Gandhi* and by Farrah Fawcett in the television film *Double Exposure: The Story of Margaret Bourke-White*.

Also behind the camera lens, John H. White, born in 1945 in Lexington, North Carolina, is the *Chicago Sun Times* photojournalist who was awarded a Pulitzer Prize in 1982 for his 'consistently excellent work on a variety of subjects.'

A recorder of historical events through the medium of the pen, rather than the camera, Theodore White, born in Boston in 1915, was one of the twentieth century's leading American political historians and journalists.

He was *Time* magazine's correspondent in China during the Second World War, his experiences there subsequently documented in his 1946 *Thunder Out of China*, but he is best known for his detailed accounts and analysis of the 1960, 1964, 1968 and 1972 U.S. presidential elections.

These were published as best-selling books, one of which, *The Making of the President*, 1960, won a Pulitzer Prize for general non-fiction.

His *Breach of Faith: The Fall of Richard Nixon*, was published eleven years before his death in 1986.

Chapter four:

On the world stage

Bearers of the White and Whyte names have also achieved fame through a colourful range of other pursuits.

The recipient of a 2010 Screen Actors Guild Lifetime Achievement Award, **Betty White** is the veteran American actress and comedian who was born in 1922 in Oak Park, Illinois.

Her best known roles include that of Sue Ann Nivens on *The Mary Tyler Moore* television show – for which she won a 1975 Emmy Award for Outstanding Support Actress in a Comedy Show – and that of Rose Nyland in *The Golden Girls*, for which she received the 1986 Emmy Award for Outstanding Lead Actress.

Born in 1904 in Paterson, New Jersey, **Alva White** was the American actress who starred in films that include the 1928 *Show Girl* and, from 1949, *Flamingo Road*; the actress, who died in 1983, has a star on the Hollywood Walk of Fame.

Best known for her role in the British television drama *Life on Mars*, **Liz White** is the actress who was born in 1979 in Rotherham, South Yorkshire, while **Karen White**, born in Philadelphia in 1965, is the American film and television actress who first came to fame in the role from 1990 to 1992 of Charmiane Brown in the television sitcom *The Cosby Show*.

Born in 1950 in London, **Shiela White** is the English actress of stage and television series that include the 1976 *I, Claudius*, while **Larry Grayson** was the stage name of the English stand-up comedian and television presenter William Sulley White, who was born in 1923 in Banbury, Oxfordshire.

The host of such popular series as *The Generation Game* and the 1975 show *Shut that Door!* – his catchphrase – he died in 1995.

From the stage to music, no less than three bearers of the White name are renowned drummers.

Born in 1930 in Glasgow, **Andy White** is the Scottish drummer who has the rare distinction as having played on one of the Beatles' hits.

This was in September of 1962 when record producer George Martin was dissatisfied with Ringo Starr's drumming on the band's first single, *Love Me Do*, and drafted in session musician White to replace him for the recording and for the B-side, *P.S. I Love You*.

The single went on to become a major international hit – but White is reported to have received only £57 for the session and does not share in any of the massive royalties that have accrued over the years.

Born in 1972 in Eltham, London, **Alan White** is the drummer best known for having played with the British rock group Oasis between 1995 and 2004.

Yet another **Alan White**, born in 1949 in Pelton, County Durham, is the drummer who, in addition to having performed with the progressive rock group Yes, also played for John Lennon's plastic Ono Band and on Lennon's *Imagine* album.

Behind the microphone, **Barry White** – born Barrenco Eugene Carter in Galveston, Texas, in 1944 – was the multi-award winning singer, songwriter, arranger and record producer who's many major hits include the 1973 *I'm Gonna Love You Just a Little Bit More, Baby* and the 1978 *Your Sweetness is My Weakness*.

He died in 2003, while to date his record sales exceed 100 million.

In contemporary rock music, **Snowy White**, born Terence White in 1948 in Devon, is the guitarist who played with Thin Lizzy from 1979 to 1981 and whose solo single, *Bird Of Paradise*, was a UK Top Ten hit in 1983.

Back across the Atlantic, Booker T. Washington White, born in Mississippi in 1906 and who died in 1977, was the blues guitarist and singer better known as **Bukka White**. A cousin of the legendary blues guitarist B.B. King, he was inducted into the Blues Hall of Fame in 1990.

In Scotland, **Tam White** is the musician and actor, born in Edinburgh in 1942, who provided the vocals for the actor Robbie Coltrane to mime his character of Big Jazza McGlone in the 1987 British television series *Tutti Frutti*.

In Scottish folk music, **Alasdair White**, born in 1983 on Lewis, in the Outer Hebrides, has been the fiddle player since 2001 with the Battlefield Band. He also enjoys a successful solo career.

An inductee of the Rock and Roll Hall of Fame and the Vocal Group Hall of Fame through his membership of the American band Earth, Wind and Fire, **Maurice White** is the singer, songwriter, arranger and record producer who was born in 1941 in Memphis, Tennessee.

Founded by White in the early 1970s, Earth, Wind and Fire, one of whose most famous hits is the

1976 *Got to Get You into My Life*, have to date sold more than 90 million albums worldwide.

From music to the highly competitive world of sport, **Jimmy White** is the English snooker player who was born in 1962 in the Tooting district of London.

Nicknamed "The Whirlwind", he began his professional career in 1980 after winning that year's Amateur World Championship, and went on to compete in the finals of six professional world championships.

Although he did not win any of these, he was at one time ranked No. 2 in the world, while in 1984 he shared the World Doubles Championship with Alex "Hurricane" Higgins.

In baseball, **Bill White** is the former first baseman who was born in 1934 in Lakewood, Florida.

Teams he played for include the New York Giants and the San Francisco Giants and, from 1966 to 1968, the Philadelphia Phillies, while from 1989 to 1994 he was president of the sport's National League – the first African American to hold the post.

On the ice, **Charlie White**, born in 1987 in Dearborn, Michigan is the American ice dancer who, along with partner Meryl Davis, won the 2009 and

2010 U.S. National Championships and a silver medal at the 2010 Winter Olympics in Vancouver.

In ice hockey, **John White**, born in 1977 in New Glasgow, Nova Scotia, is the Canadian defenceman who was a member of the New Jersey Devils team of the National Hockey League that won the prestigious Stanley Cup in 2000 and 2003.

Nicknamed "The Flying Tomato" because of his shock of red hair, **Shaun White**, born in 1986 in San Diego, is the American snowboarder who won gold in the 'halfpipe' events at both the 2006 and 2010 Winter Olympics.

On the rugby pitch, **Des White** is the former rugby league fullback recognised as having been one of New Zealand's greatest players of the game.

Born in 1927, he is remembered for having kicked a world record of eleven goals, against Australia, in 1952.

In Scotland, **Derek Whyte**, born in Glasgow in 1968, is the former player with teams that include Celtic, Aberdeen and Middlesbrough and who was a member of the national team from 1987 to 1999.

In American football, **Reggie White**, born in 1961 in Chattanooga, Tennessee, was the American defensive end who played for 15 seasons from 1984 for teams that include the Philadelphia Eagles, Green Bay Packers and Carolina Panthers.

Bearers of the White and Whyte names have also gained distinction in the creative world of literature.

Recognised as one of the greatest English language writers of the twentieth century, **Patrick White** was the British-born Australian novelist who, from 1935 until his death in 1990, produced twelve novels, two collections of novels and eight plays.

Born in 1912 in Knightsbridge, London but later moving to Sydney with his family when aged only six months, in 1973 he became the first Australian to receive the Nobel Prize for Literature – 'for an epic and psychological narrative art, which has introduced a new continent into literature.'

White, whose acclaimed novels include the 1939 *Happy Valley*, the 1957 *Voss* and the 1966 *The Solid Mandala*, used the money from his Nobel Prize to establish a trust to fund Australia's annual Patrick White Award for creative writers.

Born in India in 1906 of English parentage, Terence Hanbury White, better known as **T.H. White**, was the writer best remembered for his *The Once and Future King* series of Arthurian novels, including the

1938 *The Sword in the Stone* and the 1946 *The Candle in the Wind*.

It was after his death in 1964 that the series inspired the Broadway musical *Camelot* and the Disney animated film *The Sword in the Stone*.

A member of the American Academy of Arts and Letters, **Edmund White III.**, born in 1944 in Cincinnati, is the acclaimed American author and literary critic whose novels include the 1973 *Forgetting Elena*, while **Jack Whyte**, born in 1940, is the Scots-Canadian novelist whose work includes the Knights Templar trilogy of *Knights of the Black and White*, *Standard of Honour* and the 2009 *Order in Chaos*.

In the realms of science fiction, **James White**, born in Belfast in 1928, was the Northern Irish novelist whose books include the 1962 *Hospital Station*, the 1991 *The Silent Stars Go By* and, published in the year of his death in 1999, *Earth: Final Conflict*.

Best known for her 1936 novel *The Wheel Spins*, later memorably adapted for film by Alfred Hitchcock as *The Lady Vanishes*, **Ethel White** was the Welsh crime writer born in 1876 in Abergavenny and who died in 1944.

Winner of an honorary Pulitzer Prize in 1978,

Elwyn Brooks White, better known as **E.B. White**, was the American author of both children's and adult books who was born in 1899 in Mt. Vernon, New York.

White, who died in 1985, was the author of books that include his 1945 *Stuart Little*, later adapted as an animated film of the same name.

Every family has the odd skeleton or two rattling around in the closet, and no less so than the international family of Whites.

This is in the form of William Jack White, better known as the feared gangster of the American Prohibition era **Three Fingers White**.

Born in 1900, his nickname stemmed from a childhood accident in which he lost two fingers from his right hand – but unfortunately for his gangland rivals these did not include his rather itchy trigger finger.

Declared a public enemy in the Chicago Crime Commission report of 1923 as a member of the notorious Johnny Turrio-Al Capone crime syndicate, he was shot dead eleven years later by rival gunmen.